WRITING FOR MINECRAFTERS

Grade 3

Sky Pony Press
New York

Sky Pony Press books may be purchased in bulk at special discounts for sales promotion, corporate gifts, fund-raising, or educational purposes. Special editions can also be created to specifications. For details, contact the Special Sales Department, Sky Pony Press, 307 West 36th Street, 11th Floor, New York, NY 10018 or info@skyhorsepublishing.com.

Sky Pony® is a registered trademark of Skyhorse Publishing, Inc.®, a Delaware corporation.

Visit our website at www.skyponypress.com.

10 9 8 7 6 5 4 3 2

Library of Congress Cataloging-in-Publication Data is available on file.

Cover design by Brian Peterson
Cover illustration by Bill Greenhead

Interior illustrations by Amanda Brack
Book design by Kevin Baier

Print ISBN: 978-1-5107-4120-1

Printed in China

A NOTE TO PARENTS

When you want to reinforce classroom skills at home, it's crucial to have kid-friendly learning materials. This *Writing for Minecrafters* workbook transforms writing practice into an irresistible adventure complete with diamond swords, zombies, skeletons, and creepers. That means less arguing over homework and more fun overall.

Writing for Minecrafters is also fully aligned with National Common Core Standards for 3rd-grade writing. What does that mean, exactly? All of the writing skills taught in this book correspond to what your child is expected to learn in school. This eliminates confusion and builds confidence for greater homework-time success!

Whether it's the joy of seeing their favorite game characters on every page or the thrill of writing about Steve and Alex, there is something in this workbook to entice even the most reluctant writer.

Happy adventuring!

WRITE WHAT YOU KNOW

Look at the characters below. Finish the sentence about each Minecrafting character or mob using what you see or know. The first one is done for you.

1. Alex has _____a carrot._____ .

2. The bee is _____ .

3. The camel has _____ .

4. The chicken is _____ .

5. The armor is _____ .

6. A melon block is _____.

7. The ocelot _____.

8. The spider _____.

9. Steve is wearing _____.

10. Witches can _____.

LIBRARIAN'S GUIDE TO COLLECTIVE NOUNS

Collective nouns are words used to describe groups of items. For example, a group of fish is also called a **school** of fish.

Underline the words below that are collective nouns:

crowd	child	litter	family
swarm	kitten	book	tribe

Choose three collective nouns from the list above and use them to write sentences about Minecrafting.

1. _____

_____.

2. _____

_____.

3. _____

_____.

MORE COLLECTIVE NOUNS

Match the collective noun to the group it best describes.

1. swarm

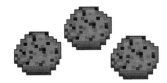

2. litter

3. pile

4. batch

5. school

6. den

FACT VS. OPINION

*A **fact** is something that can be proven true. An **opinion** is your personal feelings about a topic, or your point of view.*

Read the sentences below, and then decide whether it is a fact or an opinion. Write "F" for fact or "O" for opinion on the line.

_____ **1.** Minecraft is the best video game in the world.

_____ **2.** Minecraft can be played in Survival Mode or Creative Mode.

_____ **3.** Nether wart is needed to make a potion.

_____ **4.** Ocelots can be tamed with a fish.

_____ **5.** The ghast is the scariest of all the mobs.

_____ **6.** It's difficult to craft a pickaxe in Minecraft.

WRITE YOUR OPINION

*Which of the following mobs is the most dangerous in Minecraft? Choose one and complete the paragraph below. First you will state your **point of view** and then give three **reasons**.*

  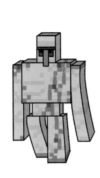 

The _____ is the most dangerous mob because

_____.

Also, it _____.

Finally, it _____.

In conclusion, _____ is the most

dangerous of all the mobs above.

QUOTE ME

Add quotation marks where they belong in the sentences below.

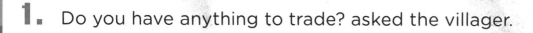

1. Do you have anything to trade? asked the villager.

2. Alex ran from the creeper yelling, It's gonna blow!

3. Steve, said Alex, I think it's time to explore the Nether.

4. After throwing her splash potion, the witch yelled, I'll get you next time.

5. This is bad, said the zombie when it noticed the sun coming out.

Write your own quotation below.

_____

_____

_____

QUOTATION MARKS

Circle the places where the quotation marks are missing or in the wrong place. Put them in the correct place.

1. What a beautiful emerald," said Steve.

2. "Let's go looking" for tonight's dinner, said Alex.

3. "Quick! Get your bow and arrow"! Steve yelled.

4. "I want to be a chicken jockey when I grow up, said the baby zombie."

5. "I have a new diamond chest plate, Steve told Alex.

9

SEQUENCE OF EVENTS

In **expository writing**, ideas, reasons, or steps are presented in a logical order. Place the sentences below in the correct order so the directions make sense.

_____ **1.** Finally, enjoy watching your snow golem shoot snowballs at your enemies!

_____ **2.** Place the second snow block on top of the first one.

_____ **3.** If you want to make a snow golem, start with two snow blocks and a pumpkin in your inventory.

_____ **4.** After you stack the snow blocks, place the pumpkin on the top.

_____ **5.** Place one snow block down.

RECIPE FOR EXPOSITORY WRITING

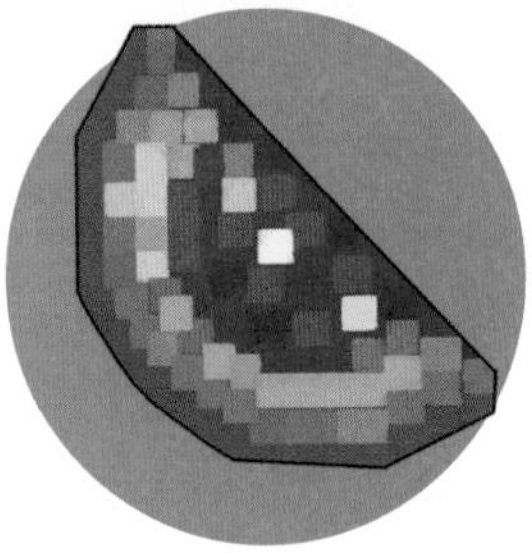

Your health bar is getting low. It's time to make a potion of Healing. Describe the steps you would take to make or get this potion and restore your health. Use some of the words in the word box to show the order in which you would do things.

First	Then	Next	Secondly
After	Later	Finally	Lastly

_____

_____

_____

_____

_____

_____

_____

_____

VERB AGREEMENT

*Verbs have to agree with their subject. Witches **brew** potion, but a single witch **brews** potion. Look at the sentences below. Choose the best verb from the word box and write it on the line. Make sure it agrees with the subject.*

build	teleport	attack	swim	shoot

1. Steve _____ a sword on his crafting table.

2. The player _____ the spider with his sword.

3. When a skeleton _____ arrows at you,

   it's best to run.

4. Endermen will _____ toward you if you make

   eye contact.

5. A dolphin usually _____ with other dolphins.

VERB AGREEMENT

(continued)

*Fix each sentence by changing the **verb** to match the subject.*
The first one is done for you.

1. Alex ~~bring~~ **brings** her golden sword with her to the End.

2. To make your flowers grows, place them in bonemeal.

3. The Enderman teleport over to Steve.

4. The players makes fishing rods from sticks and string.

5. The witch throw a splash potion.

6. The skeleton shoot many arrows.

7. The zombie prefer to live in the dark.

8. The jungle biomes has a lot of trees.

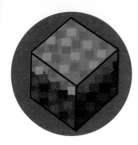

SENTENCES

A **sentence** is a group of words that tells a complete thought. All sentences begin with a **capital letter**. A statement ends with a **period**. A sentence includes a **noun**, a **verb**, and sometimes an **adjective**.

ADJECTIVE
a describing word, like *scary*

NOUN
a person, place or thing, like *creeper*

VERB
an action word, like *run*

✚ Draw a triangle around the **capital letter** that begins the sentence.

✚ Circle the **noun** (there may be more than one).

✚ Underline the **verb**.

✚ Draw a rectangle around the **adjective**.

✚ Draw a square around the **period** that ends the sentence.

1.  The heavy anvil falls on the skeleton.

2. A golden apple cures a zombie villager.

3.  A blaze shoots fireballs at players.

4. Use dye to make a yellow sheep.

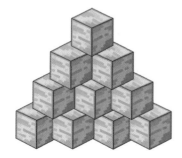 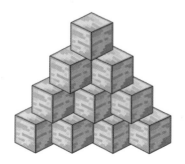 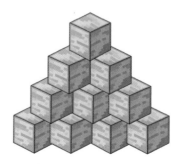

DESCRIBING IN DETAIL

Use the word box on the opposite page to help you write 5 sentences about the picture below. Remember to use capital letters at the beginning of each sentence and a period at the end.

| snow | clouds | biome | cold | wildlife |
| icy | lake | trees | igloo | |

1. _____

_____.

2. _____

_____.

3. _____

_____.

4. _____

_____.

5. _____

_____.

SILLY FILL-IN

Fill in the word blanks below. Read the story at right and add your words as you go. Did it make you laugh?

ADJECTIVE
a describing word, like *scary*

NOUN
a person, place or thing, like *creeper*

VERB
an action word, like *run*

1. _____
   VERB

2. _____
   VERB ENDING IN "ING"

3. _____
   NOUN

4. _____
   VERB ENDING IN "ING"

5. _____
   NUMBER

6. _____
   ADJECTIVE

7. _____
   FAMILY MEMBER

8. _____
   PLURAL NOUN

9. _____
   PART OF THE BODY

10. _____
    ADJECTIVE

CREEPER GOES TO A BIRTHDAY PARTY

Alex invited a friendly creeper to Steve's birthday party. When they arrived

at Steve's house, the creeper watched the kids _____ in the
                                                    VERB

backyard. He saw streamers and balloons _____ from the
                                          VERB ENDING IN "ING"

ceiling. A _____ was piled with presents, cupcakes, and
            NOUN

potion of _____ .
           VERB ENDING IN "ING"

"Hi, Steve," said Alex. "This is my new creeper friend. Happy birthday!"

"What's a birthday?" asked the creeper.

"You need some party hats," Steve said. He put _____ hats
                                                 NUMBER

on the creeper. The creeper looked _____ .
                                     ADJECTIVE

"I think your table is on fire," the creeper said after Steve's

_____ lit the _____ on the cake. The kids
FAMILY MEMBER   PLURAL NOUN

started to sing "Happy Birthday." The creeper looked frightened. Steve

handed him a piece of cake on a plate with a fork. The creeper didn't know

what the fork was for, so he used his _____ to eat. It was
                                        PART OF THE BODY

an _____ day!
    ADJECTIVE

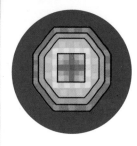

IN THE DESERT

Pretend you spawn (start in the game) in the Desert Biome. Describe how you would survive. Use details.

1. If I spawned in the desert, I would _____

_____.

2. If I needed food, I would _____

_____.

3. Finally, I would stay safe by _____

_____.

IRREGULAR PLURAL NOUNS

Rewrite the sentences. Change the noun in parentheses into a plural noun from the box and write it on the line. The first one is done for you.

torches	babies	shelves	potatoes	foxes

1. The (torch) __torches__ will light the path.

2. Arctic (fox) _____ live in the Arctic Biome.

3. The zombie family had two (baby) _____.

4. The librarian put the books on the (shelf)

_____.

5. French fries are made from (potato)

_____.

MORE IRREGULAR PLURAL NOUNS

Some nouns need an 's' on the end to be plural. Some irregular nouns do not. Circle the nouns below that don't need an 's' to describe more than one item.

Armor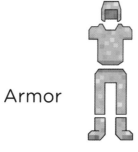

 Tree

 Sheep

Fish

Cow

Cheese

Milk

WRITE YOUR OPINION

Which mode of Minecraft is the best: Creative mode or survival mode? Write your opinion below using any or all of the phrases in the phrase box.

One way	Another way	In addition	In conclusion

_____

_____

_____

_____

_____

_____

_____

_____

COMPARE AND CONTRAST: VENN DIAGRAM

Fill in the Venn diagram with similarities and differences between the Swamp Biome and the Jungle Biome.

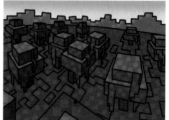

SWAMP
BIOME

JUNGLE
BIOME

BOTH

1. Write one complete sentence describing a *difference*.

_____.

2. Write one complete sentence describing a *similarity*.

_____.

SIMILARITIES AND DIFFERENCES: TABLE

Fill in the table with similarities and differences between the squid and the spider. The first line is filled in for you.

Similarities	Differences
The squid and the spider have many legs.	The squid lives in the sea and the spider lives on land.

WRITING A NARRATIVE

The four pictures below tell a story. Use the pictures to help you tell the story of Alex using a carrot to ride the pig. Write on the back of the page if needed.

1.

2.

3.

4.

_____

_____

_____

_____

_____

_____

_____

_____

_____

_____

_____

_____

IRREGULAR PAST TENSE VERBS

Fill in the blank with an irregular past tense verb from the word box below. Make sure it agrees with the subject.

ate	slept	rode	lit	made

1. Steve _____ the torches.

2. Alex _____ an apple.

3. Steve _____ in the bed.

4. Alex _____ on the pig's back.

5. Steve _____ some new potions.

USING DETAILS

Match the sentence to its more detailed version.

1. The pig turned into a zombie.

A. Alex fought off the Ender dragon with a shovel.

B. The pig turned into a zombie pigman when it was struck by lightning.

2. Alex made a sword.

3. Alex fought the dragon.

C. The horse quietly munched on the dandelion.

D. Alex created a golden sword at her crafting table.

4. The Creeper blew up.

5. The horse ate the flower.

E. The Creeper blew up when it got too close to a player.

REMEMBERING DETAILS

Steve is exploring the shipwreck site. Study the picture for a minute or two. When you think you have memorized the details, try to answer the questions on the back of the page without looking!

REMEMBERING DETAILS (continued from previous page)

Answer the questions in the space provided.

1. Name one animal in the scene besides a fish.

_____ .

2. How many masts does the ship have?

_____ .

3. What color are Steve's flippers?

_____ .

4. What is the largest animal in the scene?

_____ .

5. Which animal is in the lower right corner?

_____ .

CONTRACTIONS

*A **contraction** is two words made shorter by placing an apostrophe where letters have been omitted.*
Example: you are = you're

Write the correct contraction on the space provided. Don't forget the apostrophe!

1. Alex _____ (did not) know what to do with the

diamond.

2. Alex _____ (could not) fit her armor in the chest.

3. The butcher _____ (was not) able to sell cooked

beef.

4. The spider _____ (can not) attack you unless you

attack it first.

5. _____ (Do not) get too close to a creeper or

it will explode.

MORE CONTRACTIONS

Draw a line connecting each pair of words with its contraction.

1. I am

2. will not

3. could not

4. you are

5. do not

6. we are

7. I would

8. he is

A. we're

B. he's

C. don't

D. won't

E. couldn't

F. I'd

G. you're

H. I'm

MIX IT UP

Put the words in these mixed-up sentences in the correct order. Add a capital letter at the beginning of the sentence and a punctuation mark at the end.

1. float sky the in clouds

_____

2. hat creeper cowboy a wears the

_____

3. the wins the Enderman race

_____

4. the eats horse carrot a

_____

5. lava watch for the out

_____

6. fish puffer poisonous are

_____

7. the grow in mushrooms Nether

_____

8. do have not teeth creepers

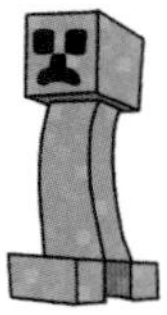

_____

9. sheep pink dyed this is

_____

10. skeletons mobs hostile are

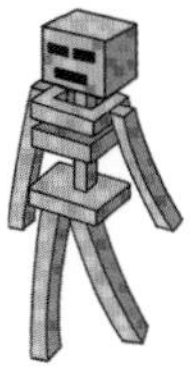

_____

WRITING A NARRATIVE

Someone hid a very valuable object in this desert temple. Write a story where you explore this mysterious temple. Describe what you find and what happens next.

Use the sentence starters below for help:

When I walked through the door of the temple, I saw . . .

Next, I . . .

Suddenly, I . . .

Then I . . .

I was shocked that . . .

Finally, I . . .

_____

_____

_____

_____

_____

_____

_____

_____

SORT THE WORDS

Sort the words in the box into the columns for nouns, verbs, and adjectives. Remember, a **noun** *is a person, place, or thing (like* igloo*). A* **verb** *is an action word (like* run*). An* **adjective** *is a describing word (like* ugly*).*

scary	pumpkin	golden	hide	mob
hostile	attack	funny	biome	villager
dig	bird	green	laugh	climb

NOUN	VERB	ADJECTIVE
_____	_____	_____
_____	_____	_____
_____	_____	_____
_____	_____	_____
_____	_____	_____
_____	_____	_____

ADDING DETAILS

*Writing is more interesting when it includes **details**. Change the sentences below. Add details to draw the reader's attention and make the writing more exciting.*

1. The mushroom is red.

_____

_____

2. The snake is scary.

_____

_____

3. Steve is sleeping.

_____

_____

4. The zombie is running away.

_____

_____

PAST TENSE

*The **past tense** describes an action that happened earlier. Write a complete sentence using the past tense to describe what Steve did. Remember to use a capital letter at the beginning and a period at the end. The first one is done for you.*

MONDAY

Steve watered his plants.

TUESDAY

_____

_____

WEDNESDAY

_____

_____

THURSDAY

_____

_____

_____

FRIDAY

_____

_____

SATURDAY

_____

_____

SUNDAY

_____

_____

PRESENT TENSE

*The **present tense** describes an action that is happening right now. Write a complete sentence using the present tense to describe what Alex does. Remember to use a capital letter at the beginning and a period at the end. The first one is done for you.*

EARLY MORNING

Alex crafts a golden sword.

LATE MORNING

_____

_____

NOON

_____

_____

AFTERNOON

_____

_____

EVENING

_____

_____

NIGHT

_____

_____

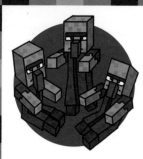

PRONOUNS

*A **pronoun** is a word that replaces a noun in a sentence. Some examples of pronouns are: I, she, he, they, it, and we. Replace the underlined nouns in the sentences below with a pronoun from the box. The first one is done for you.*

it	we	she	they	he

1. <u>Bats</u> fly at night. __They__

2. We caught <u>a creeper</u>. _____

3. <u>Villagers and I</u> ran from the blaze powder. _____

4. <u>Steve</u> is wearing armor. _____

5. <u>Alex and Steve</u> are having fun. _____

6. <u>Alex</u> packs the chest. _____

ADVERBS

An **adverb** describes actions (verbs) and other descriptive words (adjectives). Adverbs describe *where*, *when*, *and how* an action takes place. Adverbs often end in "ly" but not always. In the sentences below, circle the adverbs and underline the verbs that they describe. The first one is done for you.

1. The baby zombie <u>walked</u> (slowly.)

2. The blacksmith crossed his arms tightly.

3. The creeper exploded loudly.

4. I secretly read the enchanted book.

5. The ghast always shrieks.

6. *Write your own sentence using an adverb. Circle the adverb and underline the verb it describes.*

_____

_____

_____

INFORMATIONAL WRITING

Writing is a great way to share what you know about a topic. Informational writing can include facts, definitions, and details. It can also have a conclusion. Look at the picture below of the Forest Biome. Pretend you are explaining what the Forest Biome is to someone who has never played Minecraft. Use the sentence starters to help you organize your thoughts.

The Forest Biome is _____

_____

_____ .

The definition of a biome is _____

_____

_____ .

Another interesting fact is _____

_____

_____ .

In conclusion, _____

_____

_____ .

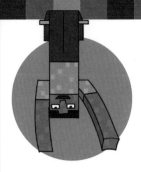

DESCRIBING IN DETAIL

Some gamer friends are at the park. Use the word box to help you write 4 sentences about the picture below. Describe the details. Remember to use capital letters at the beginning of each sentence and a period at the end.

| basketball | rainbow | slide | swing | trees |
| climb | sunny | clouds | pavement | chalk |

1. _____

_____

_____

2. _____

_____

_____

3. _____

_____

_____

4. _____

_____

_____

COMPARATIVE AND SUPERLATIVE

*Adjectives form the **comparative** by adding –er to the end of the word. Adjectives form the **superlative** by adding –est to the end of the word. An example is: sad, sadder, saddest. Fill in the chart below with the missing words. The first row has been done for you.*

Adjective	Comparative	Superlative
old	older	oldest
sharp		
	louder	
fast		tallest
	hotter	
		strongest

COMPARATIVE AND SUPERLATIVE

(continued)

Sort the words in the box into the correct category: adjective, comparative, or superlative.

scary	hardest	green	happier	funny
quickest	soft	colder	smaller	tightest
dry	wetter	brightest	angriest	braver

Adjective	**Comparative**	**Superlative**
_____	_____	_____
_____	_____	_____
_____	_____	_____
_____	_____	_____
_____	_____	

POSSESSIVE (SINGULAR)

*Fix the sentences below to make the noun **possessive**. The first one is done for you.*

A possessive noun shows ownership. Add an apostrophe and s ('s) to form the possessive of most singular nouns.

The computer of the gamer is fast.   The **gamer's** computer is fast.

1. The arrow of the skeleton is sharp.

The skeleton's arrow is sharp.

2. The shirt of Alex is green.

_____

3. The magnet of Steve is strong.

_____

4. The hut of the witch is in the forest.

_____

5. The mask of the thief is black.

_____

6. The clothes of the zombie are ripped.

_____

POSSESSIVE (PLURAL)

*Write the **possessive** form of each plural noun on the line.*
The first one is done for you.

> *A possessive noun shows ownership. To make a regular plural noun possessive, add an apostrophe (') after the s.*

The faces of the creepers are green.   The creepers' faces are green.

> *To make an irregular plural noun possessive, add an apostrophe and s ('s).*

The books of the children are heavy.   The children's books are heavy.

1. The petals of the flowers.

The flowers' petals

2. The potions of the witches.

3. The spots of the mushrooms.

4. The wool of the sheep.

5. The city of the people.

IRREGULAR PAST TENSE VERBS

Match the present tense verb on the left to its irregular past tense form on the right. The first one is done for you.

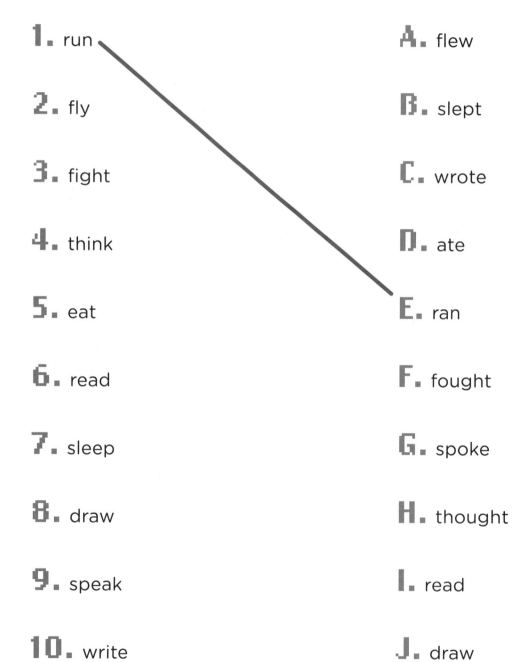

1. run
2. fly
3. fight
4. think
5. eat
6. read
7. sleep
8. draw
9. speak
10. write

A. flew
B. slept
C. wrote
D. ate
E. ran
F. fought
G. spoke
H. thought
I. read
J. draw

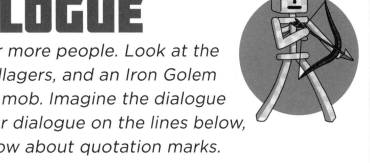

WRITING DIALOGUE

Dialogue *is speech between two or more people. Look at the picture below. Steve, Alex, some villagers, and an Iron Golem are planning an attack on a hostile mob. Imagine the dialogue among these characters. Write your dialogue on the lines below, and remember to use what you know about quotation marks.*

_____

_____

_____

_____

_____

_____

_____

_____

_____

_____

CERTIFICATE OF ACHIEVEMENT
CONGRATULATIONS

This certifies that

_____

became a

MINECRAFT WRITING BOSS

on _____.
(date)

_____

Signature

ANSWER KEY

PAGES 2-3
Write What You Know
Answers may vary, but might include the details below:

2. The bee is striped.
3. The camel has one hump.
4. The chicken is laying eggs.
5. The armor is made of diamonds.
6. A melon block is a tasty treat.
7. The ocelot is tamed with raw fish.
8. The spider spawns in darkness.
9. Steve is wearing elytra wings.
10. Witches can use splash potions.

PAGE 4
Librarian's Guide to Collective Nouns
<u>crowd</u>	child	<u>litter</u>	<u>family</u>
<u>swarm</u>	kitten	book	<u>tribe</u>

PAGE 5
More Collective Nouns

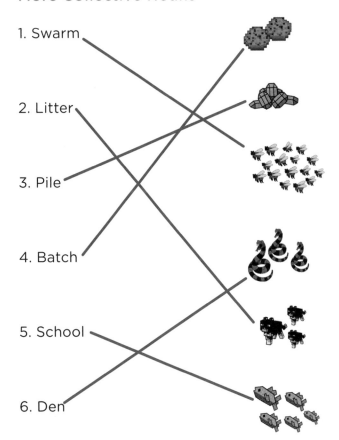

1. Swarm
2. Litter
3. Pile
4. Batch
5. School
6. Den

PAGE 6
Fact vs. Opinion

___O___ 1. Minecraft is the best video game in the world.

___F___ 2. Minecraft can be played in Survival Mode or Creative Mode.

___F___ 3. Nether wart is needed to make a potion.

___F___ 4. Ocelots can be tamed with a fish.

___O___ 5. The Ghast is the scariest of all the mobs.

___O___ 6. It's difficult to craft a pickaxe in Minecraft.

PAGE 7
Write Your Opinion
Answers will vary.

PAGE 8
Quote Me

1. "Do you have anything to trade?" asked the villager.

2. Alex ran from the creeper yelling, "It's gonna blow!"

3. "Steve," said Alex, "I think it's time to explore the Nether."

4. After throwing her splash potion, the witch yelled, "I'll get you next time."

5. "This is bad," said the zombie when it noticed the sun coming out.

PAGE 9
Quotation Marks
1. "What a beautiful emerald," said Steve.

2. "Let's go looking for tonight's dinner," said Alex.

3. "Quick! Get your bow and arrow!" Steve yelled.

4. "I want to be a chicken jockey when I grow up," said the baby zombie.

5. "I have a new diamond chest plate," Steve told Alex.

PAGE 10
Sequence of Events
__5__ Finally, enjoy watching your snow golem shoot snowballs at your enemies!

__3__ Place the second snow block on top of the first one.

__1__ If you want to make a snow golem, start with two snow blocks and a pumpkin in your inventory.

__4__ After you stack the snow blocks, place the pumpkin on the top.

__2__ Place one snow block down.

PAGE 11
A Recipe for Expository Writing
Answers will vary.

PAGE 12
Verb Agreement
1. Steve __builds__ a sword on his crafting table.

2. The player __attacks__ the spider with his sword.

3. When a skeleton __shoots__ arrows at you, it's best to run.

4. Enderman will __teleport__ toward you if you make eye contact.

5. A dolphin usually __swims__ with other dolphins.

PAGE 13
Verb Agreement
1. Alex brings her golden sword with her to the End.
2. To make your flowers grow, place them in bonemeal.
3. The Enderman teleports over to Steve.
4. The players make fishing rods from sticks and string.
5. The witch throws a splash potion.
6. The skeleton shoots many arrows.
7. The zombie prefers to live in the dark.
8. The Jungle Biomes have a lot of trees.

PAGE 15
Sentences
1. The heavy anvil falls on the skeleton.

2. A golden apple cures a zombie villager.

3. A blaze shoots fireballs at players.

4. Use dye to make a yellow sheep.

PAGES 16-17
Describing in Detail
Answers will vary.

PAGES 18-19
Silly Fill-In
Answers will vary.

PAGE 20
In the Desert
Answers will vary.

PAGE 21
Irregular Plural Nouns
1. torches
2. foxes
3. babies
4. shelves
5. potatoes

PAGE 22
More Irregular Plural Nouns

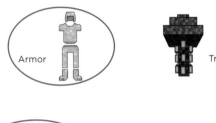

Armor   Tree

 Sheep

Cow

Fish

Milk   Cheese

PAGE 23
Write Your Opinion
Answers will vary.

PAGE 24
Compare and Contrast: Venn Diagram
Answers will vary.

PAGE 25
Similarities and Differences: Table
Answers will vary.

PAGES 26-27
Writing a Narrative
Answers will vary.

PAGE 28
Irregular Past Tense Verbs
1. lit
2. ate
3. slept
4. rode
5. made

PAGE 29
Using Details
1B
2D
3A
4E
5C

PAGES 30-31
Remembering Details
1. Shark, squid, crab
2. Two
3. Purple
4. The shark
5. The squid

PAGE 32
Contractions
1. didn't
2. couldn't
3. wasn't
4. can't
5. Don't

PAGE 33
More Contractions

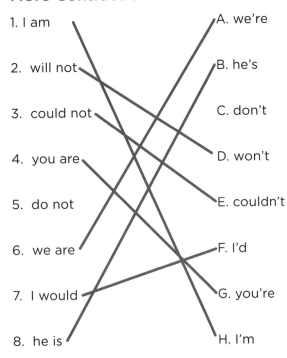

1. I am
2. will not
3. could not
4. you are
5. do not
6. we are
7. I would
8. he is

A. we're
B. he's
C. don't
D. won't
E. couldn't
F. I'd
G. you're
H. I'm

PAGES 34-35
Mix It Up

1. Clouds float in the sky.
2. The creeper wears a cowboy hat.
3. The Enderman wins the race.
4. The horse eats a carrot.
5. Watch out for the lava.
6. Puffer fish are poisonous.
7. Mushrooms grow in the Nether.
8. Creepers do not have teeth.
9. This sheep is dyed pink.
10. Skeletons are hostile mobs.

PAGES 36-37
Writing a Narrative
Answers will vary.

PAGE 38
Sort the Words

Nouns	Verbs	Adjectives
pumpkin	hide	scary
mob	attack	golden
biome	dig	hostile
villager	laugh	funny
bird	climb	green

PAGE 39
Adding Details
Answers will vary but might include the details below.

1. The bright red mushroom has white spots and a short brown stem.
2. The coiled snake is baring its fangs and looks ready to strike.
3. Steve is sleeping peacefully in his bed.
4. The zombie is fleeing the hot lava pit before it swallows him up.

PAGES 40-41
Past Tense
Answers will vary slightly but might include the details below.

MONDAY: Steve watered his plants.
TUESDAY: Steve mined some diamonds.
WEDNESDAY: He went fishing.
THURSDAY: Steve crafted a diamond sword.
FRIDAY: Steve studied on his computer.
SATURDAY: He packed a suitcase.
SUNDAY: Steve slept.

PAGES 42-43
Present Tense
Answers will vary slightly but might include the details below.

EARLY MORNING: Alex crafts a golden sword.
LATE MORNING: Alex battles the Ender dragon.
NOON: Alex mines for gold.
AFTERNOON: Alex finds a diamond.
EVENING: Alex trains her pig.
NIGHT: Alex pats her animals.

PAGE 44
Pronouns
1. They
2. it
3. We
4. He
5. They
6. She

PAGE 45
Adverbs

1. The baby zombie <u>walked</u> (slowly.)

2. The blacksmith <u>crossed</u> his arms (tightly.)

3. The creeper <u>exploded</u> (loudly.)

4. I <u>secretly</u> (read) the enchanted book.

5. The ghast (always) <u>shrieks</u>.

PAGES 46-47
Informational Writing
Answers will vary but should include a topic sentence, a definition, two facts, and a conclusion.

PAGES 48-49
Describing in Detail
Answers will vary.

PAGE 50
Comparative and Superlative

Adjective	Comparative	Superlative
old	older	oldest
sharp	**sharper**	**sharpest**
loud	louder	louder
fast	**faster**	**fastest**
tall	**taller**	tallest
hot	hotter	**hottest**
strong	**stronger**	strongest

PAGE 51
Comparative and Superlative

Adjective	Comparative	Superlative
green	happier	hardest
scary	colder	quickest
soft	smaller	tightest
funny	wetter	brightest
dry	braver	angriest

PAGE 52
Possessive (Singular)
1. The skeleton's arrow is sharp.
2. Alex's shirt is green.
3. Steve's magnet is strong.
4. The witch's hut is in the forest.
5. The thief's mask is black.
6. The zombie's clothes are ripped.

PAGE 53
Possessive (Plural)
1. the flowers' petals
2. the witches' potions
3. the mushrooms' spots
4. the sheep's wool
5. the people's city

PAGE 54
Irregular Past Tense Verbs

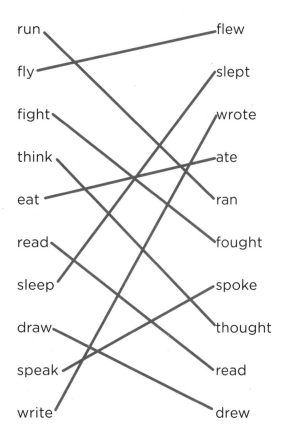

run — ran
fly — flew
fight — fought
think — thought
eat — ate
read — read
sleep — slept
draw — drew
speak — spoke
write — wrote

PAGE 55
Writing Dialogue

Answers will vary but should show correct usage of quotation marks.